# THE
# TOTALLY
# BURGERS
## COOKBOOK

# THE
# TOTALLY
# BURGERS
## COOKBOOK

*by Helene Siegel
and
Karen Gillingham*

CELESTIAL ARTS
BERKELEY, CALIFORNIA

*The Totally Burgers Cookbook* is produced by becker&mayer!, Ltd.

Printed in Singapore.

Cover design and illustration: Bob Greisen
Interior design and typesetting: Susan Hernday
Interior illustrations: Carolyn Vibbert

Library of Congress Cataloging-in-Publication Data:
Siegel, Helene.
  Totally Burgers / by Helene Siegel and Karen Gillingham.
  p.     cm.
  ISBN 0-89087-806-4
  1. Hamburgers    2. Meat substitutes    I. Gillingham, Karen.
  II. Title.
  TX749.5.B43s55      1996
  641.8′4—dc20        96-11355
                                              CIP

Celestial Arts Publishing
P.O. Box 7123
Berkeley, CA 94707

FOR JOE

# CONTENTS

# INTRODUCTION

Confession time. A number of years ago, when Helene was a fledgling cookbook editor, an idea for a hamburger cookbook crossed her desk. It had all kinds of high-flown ingredients like arugula and capers mixed into upscale meats like duck. The author suggested special delicate sauces and revolutionary new techniques for frying ground patties. A burger purist at the time, Helene just couldn't see the value in a burger that was not the essential beef, bun, and ketchup combination she grew up on. So she turned it down.

That was pre–turkey burgers and long before she had to cook dinner for a family every night of the week.

Now, while still believing in the sanctity of the all-beef burger, we have become burger realists. After all, what could be simpler than hamburgers when the gathering is casual and time is of the essence? But what to do when so many people are eating less beef than ever?

In accepting the new burger challenge our aim has been to remain true to the original concept. What makes a great burger great is still the flavor of the meat, be it beef, turkey, or chicken. To our minds, the other flavors should be there to highlight—not to dominate—that essential meatiness. A great bun, whatever toppings you may happen to love, and, of course, portability help to complete the happy equation.

The hamburger is as quintessentially American as blue jeans and rock 'n' roll, and if we can add a new burger or two to your repertoire, our efforts will not have been in vain. As they say in France, *Vive le hamburger*!

*When I was much younger and proportionately hungrier and less finicky, a minor form of bliss was going to a drive-in near school and eating two or three weird, adulterated combinations of fried beef, mayonnaise, tomato catsup, shredded lettuce, melted cheese, unidentifiable relish, and sliced onion. . . . They seemed wonderful then. Now I gag.*
—M. F. K. Fisher, The Art of Eating

# SUPERBURGERS

# THE ALL-AMERICAN BEEF BURGER

*When it comes to beef and burgers, we are purists.*
*Just give us ground chuck with 15 to 20 percent fat*
*and a good, hot frying pan and we are quite content.*

1½ pounds ground beef
2 garlic cloves, minced
salt and freshly ground pepper
olive oil for brushing
Worcestershire sauce to taste

Lightly combine beef and garlic and form four patties, handling as lightly as possible.

Brush the grill lightly with olive oil and pre-heat, or place cast-iron skillet sprinkled with salt over high heat. Season patties all over with salt and pepper.

Grill or fry until bottom is charred, keeping heat high and refraining from pressing. Flip and fry second side until charred for rare. (For medium or well-done, reduce heat to medium and cook a few minutes longer on each side.) Sprinkle with Worcestershire to taste and transfer to paper towels to drain. Serve hot on buns.

SERVES 4

---

*Modern American meaning of hamburger: chopped meat formed into cakes, cooked, and served on or in a soft bun.*

> —M. F. K. Fisher, The Art of Eating

# PICADILLO BURGER

*Serve these Mexican-style burgers topped with fire-roasted chile strips, sliced olives, and salsa for a caliente experience.*

1 tablespoon vegetable oil plus more for coating
½ cup chopped onion
½ cup diced, peeled apple
1 garlic clove, minced
1½ pounds ground beef
⅓ cup raisins, plumped in hot water for 10 minutes, and drained
dash each cinnamon, cloves, and cumin
salt and freshly ground pepper

Heat oil in large skillet over medium-high heat. Add the onion, apple, and garlic and sauté until just softened, about 1 minute. Cool.

Lightly combine the ground beef, onion-apple mixture, raisins, cinnamon, cloves, and cumin.

Season to taste with salt and pepper and gently form into patties.

Preheat the grill or place cast-iron skillet over high heat. Lightly coat with oil. Grill or fry patties until charred on bottom. Flip and finish cooking, refraining from flattening with spatula. Drain on paper towels. Serve hot on buns.

SERVES 4

---

*Burger Tips and Techniques*

*To panfry burgers, use a heavy skillet, preferably cast-iron, and place over high heat until good and hot. Sprinkle the pan with salt and, if using beef or meat that is already fatty, fry the meat in a dry pan. Coat the pan with a thin film of oil if using lean meat like chicken or turkey. Cook just until charred on bottom, flip, and cook second side until charred for rare. For medium and well-done burgers, first char and then reduce heat to medium and continue cooking a few extra minutes per side, flipping and turning two more times.*

# SIRLOIN BLUE CHEESE BURGER

*Hold the ketchup when serving these deluxe burgers—you don't want to overwhelm the excellent meat and sharp jalapeños.*

1 pound ground sirloin
2 ounces blue cheese, crumbled
1 to 2 jalapeños, minced without seeds
salt and freshly ground pepper
1 tablespoon butter, cut in 4 slices
Worcestershire sauce to taste

Lightly combine beef, blue cheese, and jalapeños. Gently form into four patties and season all over with salt and pepper.

Preheat the grill or place cast-iron skillet over high heat. Grill or fry the burgers until charred on bottom. Flip and cook second side, refraining from pressing. Top each with a dab of butter and sprinkle with Worcestershire sauce to taste. Serve hot on buns.

SERVES 4

# SMOTHERED CAJUN BURGER

*Sharp-tasting greens make these spicy burgers special enough to serve to guests.*

1½ pounds ground beef
1 tablespoon Cajun spice mix for meat
vegetable oil for coating
1 cup lightly steamed and drained greens,
    such as collards, mustard, *or* kale
Tabasco sauce
"Caramelized Onions" (see page 94)

Lightly combine the ground beef and spice mix. Gently form into patties.

Preheat the grill or place cast-iron skillet over high heat. Lightly coat with oil. Grill or fry patties until charred on bottom. Flip and finish cooking, refraining from flattening with spatula. Drain on paper towels.

Place burgers on buns. Top with greens, a dash or two of Tabasco, and "Caramelized Onions."

SERVES 4

---

*Burger Tips and Techniques*
*To broil burgers, preheat broiler and position rack about 4 inches from heat. Lightly oil tray if meat is lean and cook as per grilling, moving away from flame for longer cooking.*

# BASIC TURKEY BURGER

*With beef and cholesterol fear so prominent, turkey burgers have become a family staple.*

1½ pounds ground turkey
3 tablespoons diced onion
1½ tablespoons chopped fresh Italian parsley
garlic powder to taste
salt and freshly ground pepper
olive oil for coating
Worcestershire sauce to taste

Lightly combine turkey, onion, and parsley and form four patties. Season to taste with garlic powder, salt, and pepper.

Preheat the grill or place cast-iron skillet over high heat. Lightly coat grate or skillet with olive oil. Sear patties until blackened on bottom, refraining from pressing. Flip and cook second side until well seared for medium-rare. (For medium or well-done, reduce heat to medium and cook a few minutes longer on each side.) Sprinkle with Worcestershire to taste and transfer to paper towels to drain. Serve hot on buns.

SERVES 4

# ITALIAN TURKEY BURGER

*For Italian sausage lovers—these juicy burgers carry many of the same flavors. They would be nice with a tart Italian green like arugula as topping.*

1 pound ground turkey
½ pound ground pork
¼ cup diced onion
1 tablespoon minced garlic
2 teaspoons fennel seeds, roughly chopped
1 tablespoon plus 1 teaspoon chopped fresh basil
2 tablespoons drained, chopped sun-dried tomatoes
¼ teaspoon crushed red chile flakes
salt and freshly ground pepper
olive oil for coating

Gently combine turkey, pork, onion, garlic, fennel, basil, sun-dried tomatoes, and red chile flakes in bowl. Lightly form into patties. Season all over with salt and pepper.

Preheat the grill or place cast-iron skillet over high heat. Lightly coat grill or skillet with olive oil. Sear patties until blackened on bottom, refraining from pressing. Flip and cook second side until well seared for medium-rare. (For medium or well-done, reduce heat to medium and cook a few minutes longer on each side.) Drain on paper towels. Serve hot on buns.

SERVES 4 TO 6

# CHICKEN AND FENNEL BURGER

*Take a break from turkey with these elegant fennel-scented burgers. Leaves of watercress or radicchio would be nice on egg buns.*

1½ pounds ground chicken,
   thigh meat if possible
1½ teaspoons minced garlic
1 tablespoon fennel seeds, roughly chopped
½ teaspoon Dijon mustard
salt and freshly ground pepper
olive oil for coating

Lightly combine the chicken, garlic, fennel, and mustard. Gently form into patties. Season all over with salt and pepper.

Preheat the grill or place cast-iron skillet over high heat. Lightly coat grill or skillet with olive oil. Sear patties until blackened on bottom, refraining from pressing. Flip and cook second side until well seared for medium-rare. (For medium or well-done, reduce heat to medium and cook a few minutes longer on each side.) Transfer to paper towels to drain. Serve hot on buns.

SERVES 4

# CHICKEN-CURRANT BURGER

*Look for ground chicken-thigh meat in the meat case at the market. Dark meat is always tastier and juicier than white. These are excellent topped with tomatoes and watercress.*

3 tablespoons currants
1½ pounds ground chicken
1 tablespoon chopped fresh rosemary
2 teaspoons minced garlic
½ teaspoon grated lemon zest
salt and freshly ground pepper
vegetable oil for coating
¼ cup mayonnaise
1 tablespoon freshly squeezed lemon juice

In a small bowl, pour boiling water over the currants to cover. Let stand 10 minutes.

Lightly combine the chicken, rosemary, garlic, lemon zest, and drained currants. Season to taste with salt and pepper. Gently form into patties.

Preheat the grill or place cast-iron skillet over high heat. Lightly coat with oil. Fry or grill patties until charred on bottom. Flip and finish cooking. Drain on paper towels. Serve hot on buns.

In small bowl, combine mayonnaise and lemon juice. Use as spread.

SERVES 4

# CHINESE CHICKEN BURGER

*Use sesame seed buns, and dress these burgers
Asian-style with slices of peeled orange and
shredded napa cabbage.*

1½ pounds ground chicken
2 tablespoons minced green onions
2 tablespoons minced drained water chestnuts
1 tablespoon soy sauce
1 teaspoon sesame oil
freshly ground pepper
vegetable oil for coating
¼ cup mayonnaise
2 teaspoons rice vinegar
1 teaspoon hot Chinese mustard

Lightly combine the chicken, green onions, water chestnuts, soy sauce, sesame oil, and pepper to taste. Gently form into patties.

Preheat the grill or place cast-iron skillet over high heat. Lightly coat with oil. Fry or grill patties until charred on bottom. Flip and finish cooking. Drain on paper towels. Serve hot on buns.

Meanwhile, in a small bowl combine the mayonnaise, rice vinegar, and mustard. Use as a spread.

SERVES 4

---

*Burger Tips and Techniques*
*To grill burgers, preheat the grill and lightly coat the grate with oil. Cook as for pan directions, moving to indirect heat for medium or well-done burgers. Toast buns on grill.*

# LAMB AND FETA BURGER

*These rich, tasty burgers are delicious served on grilled buns brushed with olive oil and sprinkled with Herbes de Provence and garlic.*

1½ pounds ground lamb
1½ tablespoons minced garlic
3 tablespoons chopped fresh oregano
2 tablespoons chopped Kalamata olives
2 to 3 ounces feta cheese, crumbled
salt and freshly ground pepper
olive oil for coating

Lightly combine the lamb, garlic, oregano, olives, and cheese. Gently form into patties. Season all over with salt and pepper.

Preheat the grill or place cast-iron skillet over high heat. Lightly coat grill or skillet with olive oil. Fry or grill patties until charred on bottom. Flip and finish cooking, refraining from flattening with spatula. Drain on paper towels and serve.

SERVES 4

---

*Finely particulated meat, ground or shredded or chopped, has always been very appealing because it is so easy. It offers the full nutritional and sensory experience of meat to everyone—the young, the old, the toothless and the tired.*

—*Elizabeth Rozin,* The Primal Cheeseburger

# PORK TERIYAKI BURGER

*Serve on toasted pitas with thinly sliced red onion and bitter lettuce for a positively "wonton" experience.*

1½ pounds ground pork
2 teaspoons fresh minced ginger
2 teaspoons minced garlic
1 tablespoon chopped fresh cilantro
3 tablespoons finely diced, drained water chestnuts
3 tablespoons finely diced carrots
1½ teaspoons prepared teriyaki sauce
salt and freshly ground pepper
peanut *or* vegetable oil for coating
additional teriyaki for glaze

Lightly combine pork, ginger, garlic, cilantro, water chestnuts, carrots, and teriyaki sauce. Gently form into patties and season all over with salt and pepper.

Preheat the grill or place cast-iron skillet over high heat. Lightly coat with peanut or vegetable oil. Fry or grill patties until charred on bottom. Flip and cook second side, brushing with teriyaki. Flip to finish and brush with additional teriyaki. Drain on paper towels and serve hot.

SERVES 4

# VEAL SCHNITZEL BURGER

*Though this neo–veal schnitzel burger is technically not a burger, it is such an easy weeknight dinner we thought we'd slip it in for the veal lovers in the audience.*

1 pound ground veal
3 tablespoons minced onions
2 tablespoons chopped fresh Italian parsley
1 tablespoon finely minced anchovy fillets
salt and freshly ground pepper
1 tablespoon butter
4 eggs
4 slices rye, sourdough, or wheat toast

Lightly combine veal, onions, parsley, and anchovies. Gently form into four patties and season all over with salt and pepper.

Preheat the grill or place cast-iron skillet over high heat. Preheat oven to 200 degrees F.

Grill or fry the burgers until charred on bottom. Flip and cook second side, refraining from pressing. Transfer to ovenproof platter and keep warm in oven.

Meanwhile, melt the butter in a large nonstick pan over high heat. Break the eggs into the pan and fry, over easy or sunny-side up, to taste. Place veal burgers on toast and top each with egg. Grind some fresh pepper over egg and serve.

SERVES 4

# BREAKFAST BURGER

*Our version of the fast-food breakfast specialty sold at the store with the arches.*

1 pound pre-seasoned bulk pork breakfast
   *or* other sausage
vegetable oil for coating
4 eggs
salt and freshly ground pepper
4 large English muffins, split, lightly toasted
¼ cup shredded cheddar or jack cheese

Gently form sausage meat into patties. Place cast-iron skillet over high heat. Lightly coat with oil. Fry or grill patties until charred on bottom. Flip and finish cooking. Keep warm in 200 degrees F oven.

Wipe off pan, add a bit more oil if needed, and cook the eggs as desired. Season with salt and pepper to taste.

To serve, place sausage patties on muffin bottoms. Top each with egg and 1 tablespoon of cheese. Cover with muffin tops.

SERVES 4

# PATTY MELT SUPREME

*As denizens of Los Angeles, the city that invented it,
we dare not change the original all-beef patty melt.*

1 pound packaged ground beef
salt and freshly ground pepper
oil for coating
2 onions peeled and cut in ³⁄₈-inch rings
4 slices cheddar cheese
8 slices rye, wheat, *or* sourdough toast
butter for spreading

Remove meat from wrapping and cut in quarters. Gently shape to form flat ovals. Season generously with salt and pepper. Preheat broiler.

Arrange onion slices on baking tray and drizzle with oil. Broil, close to high flame, until charred all over, about 7 minutes. Reserve.

Place cast-iron pan over high heat. Lightly

coat with oil and fry patties until bottoms are charred, about 2 minutes. Flip and fry second side until charred. Top each with cheese, reduce heat to medium-low, and cover pan. Cook until cheese is melted.

Meanwhile, spread toast with butter. Top four slices with a hot patty. Divide onions and scatter over each. Top with toast and serve with usual condiments.

SERVES 4

---

*Burger Tips and Techniques*
*The key to a juicy burger is to purchase meat with some fat—15 to 20 percent is what we feel comfortable with these days. Handle it as lightly as possible to form the patty and do not press with the spatula to flatten while cooking. Pressing squeezes out the very juices that make a burger succulent.*

*Claims to the Hamburger Hall of Fame*

*In 1892 at the county fair in Akron, Ohio, Frank Menches runs out of sausage meat for sandwiches. He improvises with fried ground beef patties, to great acclaim.*

*In 1900 the founder of Louis' Lunch Counter in New Haven, Connecticut, Louis, invents a sandwich of thinly sliced steak trimmings shaped into a patty, thereby laying claim to the birth of the burger.*

*In the first media-reported hamburger sighting: Fletcher Davis of Old Dave's lunch counter in Athens, Texas, operates a sandwich concession on the midway at the 1904 St. Louis World's Fair. The burgerlike patties, slathered with mustard and onion, are an unalloyed hit. The New York Tribune calls the hamburger the "food of fairgoers."*

*Charlie Nagreen, a fixture at Wisconsin fairgrounds for 65 years, invents a handheld fried-beef patty so hungry fairgoers won't have to sit down to eat.*

# MEATLESS WONDERS

## SALMON-GINGER BURGER

*Serve this sparkling pink patty with watercress on thinly sliced, toasted country bread spread with a mixture of mustard and mayonnaise.*

1 pound skinless salmon fillet
1 tablespoon freshly grated ginger
1 egg yolk
½ teaspoon Dijon mustard
2 teaspoons soy sauce
½ teaspoon sesame oil
2 teaspoons vegetable *or* peanut oil
lemon wedges

Finely chop the salmon by hand. Transfer to mixing bowl with ginger.

Whisk the egg yolk in small bowl. Add mustard, soy, and sesame oil and whisk. Add to salmon and combine well. Gently form into four patties.

Heat vegetable or peanut oil in large nonstick skillet over high heat. Carefully slide patties into pan on spatula. Reduce heat to medium-high and fry until golden all over, about 4 minutes per side. Serve hot on buns with lemon wedges for sprinkling.

SERVES 4

---

*Historic Burger Eaters*
*J. Wellington Wimpy of Popeye comics*
*Jughead of Archie comics*
*Elvis Presley*
*Bil! Clinton*

# TUNA NIÇOISE BURGER

*Here is the traditional Niçoise salad served up on a bun.*

1 (12-ounce) can water-packed white tuna, drained and flaked
¼ cup dry bread crumbs
2 eggs, lightly beaten
¼ cup minced celery
1 tablespoon capers, drained
2 anchovy fillets, chopped (optional)
2 teaspoons grated lemon zest
olive oil for coating
4 large round French rolls, split, lightly grilled or toasted
mayonnaise
salt and freshly ground pepper

butter lettuce, blanched and chilled green
    bean pieces, chilled and sliced boiled pota-
    toes, hard-boiled egg slices, sliced black
    olives, tomato slices

Lightly combine tuna, bread crumbs, eggs,
celery, capers, anchovies, and lemon zest.
Gently form into patties.

Place cast-iron skillet over high heat. Lightly
coat with oil. Fry or grill patties until charred on
bottom. Flip and finish cooking.

Spread rolls with mayonnaise. On bottom
halves, layer lettuce leaves, beans, potatoes,
eggs, and olives. Top with tuna patties, another
leaf of lettuce, and tomato. Sprinkle with salt
and pepper to taste.

SERVES 4

# CRAB CAKE REMOULADE BURGER

*We like to layer shredded romaine lettuce and tomato slices on top of these luxury burgers.*

REMOULADE SAUCE
½ cup mayonnaise
2 teaspoons chopped gherkin
2 teaspoons chopped capers
1 teaspoon Dijon mustard
1 teaspoon chopped fresh parsley
½ teaspoon chopped fresh tarragon

CRAB CAKE BURGER
1½ pounds lump crabmeat
1 cup diced green, red, *or* yellow bell pepper
1 cup dry bread crumbs
1 egg, lightly beaten
1 tablespoon chopped fresh tarragon
salt, pepper, and flour for dusting
about ¼ cup vegetable oil

Combine sauce ingredients in a small bowl.

In another bowl, lightly combine the crab, diced pepper, bread crumbs, egg, and tarragon. Add salt and pepper to taste. Gently form into patties and dust with flour. Sprinkle with more salt and pepper. Place on waxed paper–lined tray and refrigerate at least 15 minutes.

In a large skillet, heat oil over medium-high heat. Add crab cakes and cook until lightly browned, about 1 minute. Turn and cook until second side is browned. Drain on paper towels.

To serve, spread sauce on rolls. Top with crab cakes, other toppings, and the remaining sauce.

SERVES 4

# POTATO-GARBANZO BURGER

*For a healthy and delicious vegetarian supper, serve
these Indian-inspired potato cakes on a bed of salad
greens or quickly sautéed spinach, and skip the bun.*

2 large Idaho potatoes, with skins
¼ cup olive oil
½ cup chopped onions
1 tablespoon minced garlic
2 teaspoons grated fresh ginger
1½ teaspoons curry powder
1 cup canned, drained garbanzo beans
½ tablespoon salt
freshly ground pepper

Place the potatoes in a large saucepan. Cover
generously with water, bring to a boil, reduce to
a simmer, and cook, uncovered, until done, 45
minutes. Drain and chill.

Meanwhile, heat 1½ tablespoons of the oil in a small skillet over medium heat. Sauté the onions, garlic, ginger, and curry until onions are soft. Chill.

Purée the garbanzos in food processor or blender.

When cool enough to handle, peel potatoes and grate by hand. In large bowl, combine potatoes, onion mixture, garbanzos, salt, and pepper. Gently form into six to eight patties. (Patties may be stored in the refrigerator, covered with plastic, up to 8 hours.)

To cook, preheat oven to 250 degrees F. Pour a tablespoon of oil into large nonstick skillet and place over medium heat. Slide patties into hot oil and fry, adding more oil as necessary, until golden brown on both sides. Transfer to heatproof platter and bake 20 minutes. Serve hot.

SERVES 6 TO 8

# WILD MUSHROOM BURGER

*Mushrooms and potatoes share a natural affinity. You may wish to omit the bun and serve on a tart green salad.*

1 large Idaho potato, with skin
¼ cup olive oil
⅓ cup chopped shallots
1 pound assorted wild mushrooms, cleaned and sliced
salt and freshly ground pepper
1 tablespoon chopped fresh sage

Place the potato in a large saucepan. Cover generously with water, bring to a boil, reduce to a simmer, and cook, uncovered, until done, 45 minutes. Drain and chill.

Heat 2 tablespoons of the oil in large skillet over medium-high heat. Sauté the shallots 1 minute. Add mushrooms and sauté with salt and pepper until tender, about 7 minutes. Place on plate and chill.

When cool, peel potato and grate by hand. Combine in bowl with cooled mushrooms and sage. Gently form into four patties and reserve in the refrigerator 1 hour.

To cook, preheat oven to 350 degrees F. Heat remaining oil in large nonstick skillet over medium-high heat. Fry patties until golden brown and crisp on both sides. Transfer to baking sheet and bake 15 minutes. Serve hot.

SERVES 4

# GARDEN LENTIL BURGER

*These vegetarian burgers were inspired by a favorite beachside cafe in Venice, California—Figtree's. Serve on toasted pita with the usual accompaniments.*

1 cup green lentils
2 tablespoons olive oil
½ cup chopped onions
2 teaspoons minced garlic
1 teaspoon freshly grated ginger
¾ cup walnuts
1 zucchini, finely shredded
1 large carrot, peeled and finely shredded
¼ cup sesame seeds
salt and freshly ground pepper

Place the lentils in medium saucepan. Cover generously with water. Bring to a boil, reduce to a simmer, and cook, uncovered, until tender, about 25 minutes. Drain and chill.

Heat 1 tablespoon of the oil in a small skillet over medium heat. Sauté the onions, garlic, and ginger until onions are soft. Chill.

Combine half of the chilled lentils and walnuts in blender and purée.

In large bowl, combine remaining lentils, onion mixture, zucchini, carrot, sesame seeds, puréed nut mix, salt, and pepper. Gently form into eight patties.

To cook, preheat oven to 350 degrees F. Heat remaining oil in large nonstick skillet over medium-high heat. Sauté the patties until golden on both sides, about 10 minutes total. Carefully transfer to baking sheet or platter. Bake to heat through, about 10 minutes. Serve hot.

SERVES 8

# ASIAN TOFU BURGER

*These succulent tofu patties are bound to dispel any lingering doubts concerning that high-protein food's delicious nature.*

vegetable oil for coating
1 (19-ounce) block firm tofu, in ½-inch slices
    across width
4 green onions, sliced
1½ teaspoons minced peeled ginger
2 tablespoons sesame seeds
½ cup light soy sauce
mayonnaise
alfalfa *or* bean sprouts

In a large skillet, heat oil over medium-high heat. Add tofu, onions, ginger, sesame seeds, and soy sauce. Cook 3 minutes, carefully turning tofu once, adding a little more soy sauce or water if tofu sticks.

Divide tofu and stack two or three slices on mayonnaise-coated rolls. Top with sprouts and serve.

SERVES 4

---

*It would seem, after a considerable amount of random research that has spanned a couple of decades, that there is no concretely documented evidence of the precise moment the first hamburger came into evidence.*
—Craig Claiborne, food critic

# GRILLED PORTOBELLO BURGER

*Large, meaty, dark brown portobellos are the filet mignon of the nineties.*

½ cup olive oil
6 tablespoons white wine vinegar
1 garlic clove, minced
1 tablespoon chopped fresh oregano
1 tablespoon sugar
4 large portobello mushroom caps
salt and freshly ground pepper
1 pound loaf sturdy Italian bread, cut in
    4 sections, split and lightly grilled or toasted
½ cup prepared roasted red peppers
arugula leaves

In bowl, combine oil, vinegar, garlic, oregano, and sugar. Add the mushrooms and evenly coat. Let stand at least 15 minutes, turning occasionally.

Drain mushrooms, transferring marinade to small, heavy saucepan. Set over medium heat and bring to simmer 2 minutes.

Preheat the grill or broiler. Lightly coat grate with oil. Grill or fry mushrooms until charred. Flip and finish cooking.

To serve, place mushrooms on bread, season to taste, and top with roasted peppers. Drizzle with warm marinade and top with arugula leaves. Top sandwich and serve.

SERVES 4

---

*I would gladly pay you Tuesday for a hamburger today.*
— J. Wellington Wimpy of "Popeye" fame

# BROWN RICE BURGER

*We like to serve these totally healthy burgers with the usual suspects: ketchup, mayonnaise, lettuce, and tomato.*

3 tablespoons vegetable oil
2 garlic cloves, minced
½ teaspoon each, dried sage and thyme
¾ cup brown rice
1½ cups vegetable broth
⅔ cup dry bread crumbs plus more for coating
¼ cup minced green onions
2 tablespoons soy sauce
1 egg, lightly beaten
freshly ground pepper

Heat 1 tablespoon of oil in a heavy medium saucepan, over medium-high heat. Sauté the garlic, sage, and thyme less than 1 minute. Stir in rice to coat completely. Add the broth and bring to boil. Cover, reduce heat, and simmer about 40 minutes or until rice is tender. Transfer to bowl of food processor and cool slightly. Add bread crumbs, onions, soy sauce, egg, and pepper and process to blend. Form into patties. Lightly coat with bread crumbs. Refrigerate, on waxed paper–lined tray, 30 minutes.

In a large skillet, heat the remaining oil over medium-high heat. Add the patties and cook 4 minutes. Turn and cook 4 minutes longer. Serve hot on buns.

SERVES 4

# BLACK BEAN BBQ BURGER

*Smoky barbecue sauce and earthy black beans are a match made in heaven.*

2 (15-ounce) cans black beans, well drained
2 tablespoons chopped cilantro (optional)
1 small jalapeño pepper, stemmed, seeded, and minced
salt and freshly ground pepper
cornmeal for coating
2 tablespoons vegetable oil
4 thin slices jack cheese (optional)
prepared barbecue sauce
"Quick Confetti Corn Relish" (see page 79)

Place half of the beans in small bowl and mash to a smooth paste. Stir in remaining beans along with cilantro and jalapeño. Season to taste with salt and pepper. Form into patties. Dip in corn-meal to coat lightly. Refrigerate, on waxed paper–lined tray, at least 30 minutes.

In a large skillet, heat the oil over medium heat. Carefully add the bean patties and sauté about 1 minute. Carefully turn and sauté 1 minute longer or until heated through. Top with cheese slices, if desired.

To serve, top patties with barbecue sauce and corn relish and serve on buns.

SERVES 4

### The Burger Business

*The first hamburger chain was White Castle, the turreted restaurant featuring small, square burgers, that opened in 1927. Since eating out was not the everyday occurrence it is today, the public had to be convinced about the rightness of leaving home for dinner. J. Walter Anderson, the chain's founder, promoted the health qualities and cleanliness of his product by placing the grill in front of the counter for everyone to see and offering take-out burgers, hygienically wrapped in paper and packed in bags. As the slogan said, "Buy 'em by the sack."*

# CLASSIC
# ACCOMPANIMENTS

# HOMEMADE BUNS

*Impress the guests at your next barbecue with these homemade hamburger buns.*

³/₄ cup warm water
2 tablespoons sugar
2 (¼-ounce) packages dry yeast
1 cup milk, room temperature
⅓ cup vegetable shortening
2 teaspoons salt
2 eggs
about 5 cups all-purpose flour
sesame seeds for topping (optional)

Place water in bowl of electric mixer. Add sugar and yeast, stir, and let sit until foamy, about 10 minutes.

Add milk, shortening, salt, and 1 egg and lightly beat just to break up fats. Add 2 cups of the flour and beat until smooth. Gradually add remaining flour, beating to combine. Lightly knead the shaggy dough on a counter, cover with a towel, and let rest 20 minutes.

Return to mixer with dough hook or knead by hand until smooth and elastic, 5 to 10 minutes. Transfer to large coated bowl, cover with towel, and let rise until doubled, about 1 hour.

Punch dough down, transfer to floured board, and divide into 16 pieces. Lightly knead each into a ball, press between palms to flatten, and place on coated baking sheets. Cover with towels and let rise about 45 minutes. Preheat oven to 400 degrees F.

Beat remaining egg for wash. Brush on buns, sprinkling tops with sesame seeds if desired. Bake until golden, 20 to 25 minutes. Cool on racks and split to serve.

MAKES 16

# FRIED ONION RINGS

*Beer is the secret ingredient in these ethereal onion rings.*

¾ cup all-purpose flour
1 teaspoon sugar
½ teaspoon salt
1 teaspoon baking powder
½ teaspoon cayenne
1 cup beer, room temperature
3 large onions
vegetable oil for deep frying

Combine flour, sugar, salt, baking powder, and cayenne in mixing bowl. Pour in beer and whisk until smooth. Cover and set aside at room temperature 1 hour.

Pour oil into a large pot or deep fryer to a depth of 5 inches and bring to deep-fry temperature, 350 degrees F. Peel onions and cut across width into ¼-inch slices. Separate into rings.

Working with a handful at a time, dip rings into batter and shake off excess. Fry until golden brown, being careful not to crowd the pan. Transfer with slotted spoon to paper towels to drain. Sprinkle with salt and serve hot.

SERVES 6

# LES FRITES

*We, too, rely on frozen french fries for ordinary meals, but when the occasion is stellar nothing beats homemade.*

baking potatoes, peeled
vegetable oil for frying
salt to taste

Cut potatoes into matchsticks using 6-mm julienne blade of food processor or a mandoline.

Pour oil into deep fryer or large pot to depth of 5 inches. Bring to deep-fry temperature, 350 degrees F. Fry potatoes, a handful at a time, until golden and crisp. Drain on paper towels, sprinkle with salt, and serve hot.

### The McDonald's Franchise

*McDonald's didn't invent the burger business, they just perfected it. What began with the McDonald brothers in a tiny hot dog stand near the racetrack in Arcadia, a suburb of Los Angeles, became a worldwide business operation under the aegis of Ray Kroc, a former milkshake machine salesman who bought the rights to sell the franchise nationally in 1954.*

*An astute businessman, with one eye on his bottom line and another on his beef, he focused on delivering a reliable, inexpensive, prepacked and dressed beef patty to his customers as quickly as possible. His famous motto to employees—"Keep it simple, stupid"—best sums up his philosophy of keeping a hungry public happily in hamburgers.*

# GREEK POTATO SALAD

2 pounds red potatoes, thinly sliced with skins
¼ cup red wine vinegar
1 teaspoon Dijon mustard
⅓ cup olive oil
salt and freshly ground pepper
½ red onion, thinly sliced
2 tablespoons capers, drained
½ cup chopped fresh oregano *or* Italian parsley
Tabasco to taste

Rinse potatoes in cold water to remove starch. Bring a large pot of salted water to a boil. Add potatoes, bring water back to a boil, and cook just until done in center, about 5 minutes.

Meanwhile, in large mixing bowl, whisk together red wine vinegar, mustard, olive oil, salt, and pepper.

Drain potatoes in colander and quickly rinse with cold water. Add potatoes to dressing and toss to coat evenly. Add onions, capers, and oregano or parsley. Toss to combine, and adjust seasonings with salt, pepper, and Tabasco. Serve at room temperature and store leftovers in the refrigerator.

SERVES 6

# PAN-FRIED POTATOES

*Here are some easy-to-make, crisp brown potatoes that are also delightful with eggs for breakfast.*

4 large Idaho potatoes, peeled and cut in
　½-inch cubes
¼ cup olive oil
2 sprigs fresh rosemary leaves, chopped,
　*or* ½ teaspoon dried
salt and freshly ground pepper

Bring a large pot of salted water to a boil. Add potatoes and cook 5 minutes, once water returns to a boil. Drain and pat dry with paper towels.

Heat the oil in a large nonstick skillet over high heat. Add potatoes, in single layer, and cook until bottom is golden brown. Sprinkle with rosemary, turn, and cook another 10 minutes, until second side is golden and crisp. Season to taste with salt and pepper and serve hot.

SERVES 4 TO 6

---

*The Word*
*"Hamburger" entered the American lexicon in the early 19th century as a name for broiled, chopped steak cooked in the traditional style of the port city of Hamburg, Germany.*

# BETTY'S CLASSIC POTATO SALAD

*From Karen's mom, an all-American classic summer salad.*

1 pound boiling potatoes, boiled, peeled, and
    diced
¼ cup diced white *or* red onion
¼ cup thinly sliced celery
2 tablespoons sweet pickle relish
½ cup mayonnaise
2 teaspoons prepared mustard
½ teaspoon celery seed
salt and freshly ground pepper
2 hard-cooked eggs, peeled and sliced or
    chopped

In a large bowl, combine the potatoes, onions, celery, and pickle relish.

In a small bowl, blend the mayonnaise, mustard, celery seed, salt, and pepper to taste. Add to potato mixture and toss to coat thoroughly. Chill as long as overnight. Before serving, toss again and garnish with eggs.

SERVES 4 TO 6

---

*The average American consumes three burgers a week, for a grand total of about 30 pounds of ground meat a year.*

—*Jeffrey Tennyson*, Hamburger Heaven

# GARLIC-ROASTED POTATO SALAD

1 pound baby red potatoes, quartered
12 to 16 garlic cloves, peeled
¼ cup olive oil
1 tablespoon fresh thyme leaves
1 tablespoon white wine vinegar
¼ cup sliced green onions
1 cup peas *or* 1-inch lengths asparagus,
    blanched
salt and freshly ground pepper

Preheat oven to 400 degrees F.

Combine potatoes with enough water to cover in a large saucepan. Bring to a boil, reduce to a simmer, and cook about 5 minutes. Drain.

In a shallow roasting pan, toss potatoes and garlic with olive oil. Roast about 15 minutes. Sprinkle with thyme leaves and roast another 5 to 10 minutes or until soft when pierced with fork. Remove from oven and cool. Transfer to a bowl and add the vinegar, tossing to coat. Add the green onions and, if desired, peas or asparagus. Season to taste with salt and pepper. Serve warm or at room temperature.

Serves 4 to 6

# CARROT CRANBERRY SALAD

*This pretty orange-and-red salad is a delightful mix of tart and sweet. It makes excellent picnic food.*

8 cups finely shredded carrots
(about 10 carrots)
1 cup dried cranberries, roughly chopped
½ cup cider vinegar
4 teaspoons honey
salt to taste

In a large mixing bowl, combine carrots and cranberries.

In small bowl, whisk together vinegar, honey, and salt. Pour over carrot mixture and toss well. Store in refrigerator.

MAKES 8 CUPS, 6 TO 8 SERVINGS

## QUICK CONFETTI CORN RELISH

3 cups corn kernels
1 red bell pepper, seeded and diced
1 green bell pepper, seeded and diced
3 tablespoons diced red onion
1 bunch fresh chives, sliced
¼ cup red wine vinegar
⅓ cup olive oil
salt, freshly ground pepper, and Tabasco to
    taste

Blanch corn in rapidly boiling salted water until water returns to a boil. Drain and rinse with cold water. Transfer to mixing bowl. Add bell peppers, onion, and chives and mix.

In small bowl, whisk together vinegar, oil, salt, pepper, and 2 or 3 dashes Tabasco. Pour over corn mixture, toss well, and serve or store in the refrigerator.

MAKES 3½ CUPS

# GARLIC DILL PICKLES

*These were inspired by chef Mary Sue Milliken.*

15 Kirby *or* pickling cucumbers
16 garlic cloves, peeled

PICKLING LIQUID

3 cups water
2 cups white vinegar
¼ cup coarse salt
2 tablespoons sugar
1 teaspoon black peppercorns
2 cloves
1 bay leaf
½ teaspoon ground ginger

Bring a large pot of water to a boil. Add cucumbers and garlic, immediately remove from heat, and drain. Rinse with cold water and transfer to a large container.

Combine pickling liquid ingredients in saucepan and bring to a boil. Pour hot liquid over cucumber mixture and set aside to cool. Press down solids, cover with plastic wrap, and let stand at room temperature 1 day. Transfer pickles with their juice to sealed containers and store in the refrigerator.

MAKES 15

# REFRIGERATOR BREAD AND BUTTER PICKLES

2 cups sliced pickling cucumbers *or* Kirbys
1 large onion, sliced
1 tablespoon salt
⅔ cup brown sugar, packed
¼ teaspoon turmeric
1 teaspoon mustard seeds
½ teaspoon celery seeds
¾ cup cider vinegar

In a large bowl, combine the cucumbers, onion, and salt. Cover and let stand about 2½ hours.

In a heavy medium saucepan, mix the brown sugar, turmeric, mustard seeds, celery seeds, and vinegar. Boil 3 to 4 minutes.

Meanwhile, transfer the cucumber mixture to a colander and drain. Rinse well with cold water. Add to brown sugar mixture and return to boil. Remove from heat and cool 30 minutes. Store in sealed containers in the refrigerator.

MAKES ABOUT 1 PINT

# TRIPLE THREAT RED SLAW

1 small head red cabbage, shredded
½ cup canned shredded beets, drained, liquid
    reserved
¼ cup minced red onion
2 tablespoons red wine vinegar
2 tablespoons brown sugar, packed
½ cup vegetable oil
½ teaspoon caraway seeds
salt and freshly ground pepper

In a large bowl, combine the cabbage, beets, and onion.

In a small bowl, combine 1 tablespoon reserved beet juice, vinegar, and brown sugar. Gradually whisk in the oil. Stir in caraway seeds and season to taste with salt and pepper. Pour over cabbage mixture, tossing to coat thoroughly. Cover and refrigerate 3 hours or overnight. Toss again just before serving.

SERVES 4 TO 6

---

*Rich Relations*
*Salisbury steak—or ground steak shaped in a large, flat patty and broiled—was introduced as a diet food by London doctor J. H. Salisbury.*

# COOL WHITE COLE SLAW

1 small head green cabbage, shredded
2 golden delicious apples, peeled, cored, and
   grated
½ cup golden raisins, plumped in hot water
   and drained (optional)
¼ cup minced onion
2 tablespoons apple cider vinegar
2 tablespoons honey
¾ cup mayonnaise
1 teaspoon celery seeds
salt and freshly ground pepper

In a large bowl, combine the cabbage, apples, raisins, and onion.

In a small bowl, blend the vinegar and honey. Stir in the mayonnaise and celery seeds until smooth. Add to cabbage mixture and toss to coat thoroughly. Season to taste with salt and pepper. Chill as long as overnight. Toss again just before serving.

SERVES 4 TO 6

# COWBOY BEANS

2 tablespoons vegetable oil
½ cup chopped onion
2 garlic cloves, minced
1 (4-ounce) can diced mild green chiles
2 (15-ounce) cans small red beans, drained
6 ounces beer
1 large tomato, seeded and diced
salt and freshly ground pepper
chopped cilantro (optional)

In a large saucepan, heat the oil over medium-high heat. Sauté the onion and garlic until tender. Add the chiles and cook 1 minute longer. Stir in the beans and beer. Bring to a boil, reduce to a simmer, and cook 5 minutes. Stir in the tomato and cook 1 minute longer. Season to taste with salt and pepper. Sprinkle with cilantro, if desired, and serve.

SERVES 4 TO 6

# LUNCH COUNTER MILK SHAKE

*To be young, gifted, and not to have to count calories—the classic American burger beverage.*

1 scoop vanilla ice cream
1 cup milk
2 tablespoons chocolate syrup

Place serving glasses in freezer to chill. Combine ingredients in blender and purée at high speed until smooth and thick, about 1 minute. Pour and serve.

SERVES 2

# TIP-TOP TOPPINGS

# SAUTÉED MUSHROOMS

4 tablespoons butter
½ cup finely diced onions *or* shallots
1 pound white mushrooms, trimmed and
    thinly sliced
salt and freshly ground pepper
lemon juice to taste

Melt the butter in a large skillet over medium heat. Sauté the onions or shallots until soft. Add mushrooms, turn heat to high, and cook until wilted and brown and the liquid in the pan is evaporated, about 8 minutes. Season to taste with salt, pepper, and lemon juice. Serve over burgers.

SERVES 4

# HOMEMADE KETCHUP

*Chicago food editor and writer Bev Bennett's home-grown ketchup, for finer-than-fine occasions.*

1 tablespoon olive oil
4 shallots, minced
1 tablespoon grated fresh ginger
6 plum tomatoes, peeled, seeded, and diced
2 tablespoons cider vinegar
2 tablespoons honey
6 cloves
¼ teaspoon cinnamon
1 teaspoon each salt and freshly ground pepper

Heat oil in medium saucepan over medium-high heat. Sauté shallots and ginger until soft, about 4 minutes. Add remaining ingredients. Bring to a boil, reduce to a simmer, and cook, stirring frequently, until thickened, 20 minutes. Purée in blender or mash with potato masher. Chill and serve.

MAKES 1 CUP

---

*In 1902 the first American recipe appeared for hamburger in* Mrs. Rorer's Cookbook. *It called for beef to be hand ground twice and then combined with onion and pepper.*

## CARAMELIZED ONIONS

1 tablespoon olive oil
2 large onions, thinly sliced
2 tablespoons red wine *or* balsamic vinegar
1 teaspoon sugar
salt and freshly ground pepper

In a large skillet, heat oil over medium-high heat. Sauté the onions, stirring frequently, about 15 minutes or until very soft. Reduce heat to low and add vinegar and sugar. Cook until liquid is nearly evaporated, about 20 minutes, stirring occasionally. Season to taste with salt and pepper and serve hot over burgers.

MAKES ABOUT 1 CUP, ENOUGH FOR 4 BURGERS

*Mothers and dads, if your children like hamburgers, let
them eat as many . . . as they want. They are made by
our intelligent, conscientious, and highly trained young
men in clean, sanitary surroundings. They are as pure
and wholesome as any food in the world can be.*
      *—White Castle ad*

# CONVERSIONS

## LIQUID
1 Tbsp = 15 ml
½ cup = 4 fl oz = 125 ml
1 cup = 8 fl oz = 250 ml

## DRY
¼ cup = 4 Tbsp = 2 oz = 60 g
1 cup = ½ pound = 8 oz = 250 g

## FLOUR
½ cup = 60 g
1 cup = 4 oz = 125 g

## TEMPERATURE
400° F = 200° C = gas mark 6
375° F = 190° C = gas mark 5
350° F = 175° C = gas mark 4

## MISCELLANEOUS
2 Tbsp butter = 1 oz = 30 g
1 inch = 2.5 cm
all-purpose flour = plain flour
baking soda = bicarbonate of soda
brown sugar = demerara sugar
confectioners' sugar = icing sugar
heavy cream = double cream
molasses = black treacle
raisins = sultanas
rolled oats = oat flakes
semisweet chocolate = plain chocolate
sugar = caster sugar